To Speak to Each Day in Its Own Language

To Speak to Each Day
in Its Own Language

Poems by

Melissa Huff

© 2025 Melissa Huff. All rights reserved.
This material may not be reproduced in any form, published,
reprinted, recorded, performed, broadcast,
rewritten, or redistributed without
the explicit permission of Melissa Huff.
All such actions are strictly prohibited by law.

Cover design by Shay Culligan
Cover art "Sightings" by Melissa Huff
Author photo by Sarah Lincoln

ISBN: 978-1-63980-833-5

Kelsay Books
502 South 1040 East, A-119
American Fork, Utah 84003
Kelsaybooks.com

Acknowledgments

Thank you to the editors of the following journals, where many of the poems in this collection first appeared, sometimes in earlier forms:

Amethyst Press: "Fern Room, Lincoln Park Conservatory"
Amethyst Review: "Bhutan—Notes from a Journey," "Each Moment a Bird," "Shoreline"
Blue Heron Review: "Storehouse," "Talking with Trees," "Wakening"
Brush Talks: A Journal of China: "Promises Made by a Chinese Landscape Painting When You Enter at Its Feet"
East on Central: "Conversation with Bashō," "Imagine Doing the Same"
Green Ink Poetry: "We Are Here, Though Our Glory Be Brief"
Gyroscope Review: "Aubade," "Call and Response," "Lesson in Aging"
Halfway Down the Stairs: "Pilgrimage, Early March"
National Federation of State Poetry Societies: "Riverspeak"
The Nature of Our Times: "Evidence of Fire," "Hidden Knowledge," "Learning from Landscape"
Northern Colorado Writers: "Advanced Civilizations 101"
The Orchards Poetry Review: "Metamorphosis"
Origami Poems: "Air Songs," "Come to Me in April," "Spring Is a Strong Verb"
Persimmon Tree: "Putting My Mind Down for a Nap"
RockPaperPoem: "Against a Bleached Evening Sky"
Snapdragon: A Journal of Art and Healing: "It All Happens Here"
WildaMorrisBlogspot.com: "Where Do All the Colors Go"
Winterwolf Press: "Belonging"

I wish to thank the members of Plumb Line Poets for their creative insights and workshop prowess, which helped make my poetry so much better than it would have been without them.

I am grateful to the readers of my first draft, fellow poets Patrice Boyer Claeys, Carol Sadtler and Kirsten Morgan, for the time they took to provide valuable comments and new perspectives.

Special thanks to Kathleen Willard, who encouraged me to think outside the box and enabled me to see my manuscript, as well as the poems in it, with fresh eyes.

Much appreciation also goes out to C. E. Janecek, whose editing skills, structural thinking, and experience navigating the poetry publishing world helped to shape this book.

Contents

Honeysuckle   13

I. Talking with Trees

Spring Is a Strong Verb	17
Come to Me in April	18
Lesson in Aging	20
Advanced Civilizations 101	21
Imagine Doing the Same	22
We Are Here, Though Our Glory Be Brief	23
Air Songs	24
Storehouse	26
Pomegranate	27
Where Do All the Colors Go	28
Talking with Trees	29
Doggedness	30
Sakura	31

II. Threshold

Fern Room, Lincoln Park Conservatory	35
In Search of Magic	37
The Statue in the Orchid House Becomes My Teacher	38
Threshold	40
Walking Meditation	41
Hidden Knowledge	42
A Language of Sensing	43
Undercurrents	44
Learning from Landscape	45
Promises Made by a Chinese Landscape Painting, When You Enter at Its Feet	46

Against a Bleached Evening Sky   47
Skybound   48
Aubade   49

III. Inhaling Light

Across the Water   53
Solstice Promise   54
Inhaling Light   55
It All Happens Here   57
Inner Body   59
Putting My Mind Down for a Nap   60
Wick   62
Wakening   63
Musings on the Body   65
Paradelle for La Loba   66
Evidence of Fire   67

IV. The Calm Embedded in Forward Motion

Riverspeak   71
Pilgrimage, Early March   72
Horizon   73
Bhutan—Notes from a Journey   74
Prayer Ghazal   79
Trying on Cultural Symbols in Taipei 80
Call and Response   82
Shoreline   83
Each Moment a Bird   85
Metamorphosis   86
Conversation with Bashō   87
Belonging   88

Honeysuckle

after Jane Kenyon's poem, "Evening Sun"

Why does the headiness
           of honeysuckle
pull me back
   to my childhood?
            Its dense fragrance
would drench me
   with the scent
            of summer's longing
whenever I ran to the foot
         of the climbing tree
where this unfettered
   vine flourished.
            I'd inhale its perfume
before wedging one sneaker
         against rough bark
and swinging up
   out of its reach.
           I laughed with Kim
as we tried to make
   garlands of it, weaving
            the delicate yellow
and white that spilled
   from ribbons of green.
           Did I know then
that I would try to intertwine
          life's found materials
with strands of curiosity
   that I might create
            garlands of meaning?

I. Talking with Trees

Spring Is a Strong Verb

Do not suppose it gentle
this season of greening
when bundled fibers gather
their juices until girdled
with power they push
through the earth drive
into the sky wielding buds
filled with fierce energy
that defy gravity until
time to unfold and hold
the strength of the sun.

Come to Me in April

Wrap me in the first strong,
supple leaves of spring—
let their yellow-green
infuse me.

Sing to me those songs
embedded in the breeze—
rock me to the rhythm
of their breath.

Feed me eager buds
before they open—
newness plucked with ease
from fertile earth.

Fill my lungs
with younger air—
a sweetness seeping out
of winter's fringe.

Watch me run
through rain-soaked streams—
rinsing out debris
from seasons left behind.

Walk with me
along the furrowed edge
of fields in which
tomorrow grows.

Sit with me
and let us gather
sips of sunlight—
gold upon our lips.

Lesson in Aging

I spread their colors
across the counter—tulips
in hues of lemon, lilac,
plum and persimmon—
then scoop them up,
slake their thirst, let them
chatter to each other.
They tilt their heads, laugh
from their bellies, begin
to open themselves to life.
As they age, they widen
their scope, become more
generous, acquire a graceful
drape. Their edges begin
to darken, turn inward
until, one by one, each
petal loosens its hold,
gives in to gravity,
leaving—strewn
across my counter—
curled flakes of color,
still laughing.

Advanced Civilizations 101

Today's lesson:

Trees really do communicate with each other. With scent. With underground networks of tiny fungal filaments. Dense intertwining root systems pulse with electrical messages. Chemical dispatches. The talking has begun. Don't misunderstand—you'll get no gossip from these gracious creatures. No backbiting. No passive-aggressive language. Far from it. In fact, they send water and nutrients to nurture ailing companions. Emit gases to signal danger. Disperse pheromones throughout the air—scent signals that summon good insects to attack the bad. So next time you find yourself in an ancient grove, consider it a classroom for learning kindness.

Imagine Doing the Same

yesterday's peony bud
hard-packed   protected

today   lifts its face
lets go the cloak

that kept it dreaming   of tomorrow's light
offers its petals

the chance to live   and die
sun-drunk   rinsed by rain

buffeted   and buoyed
by spirited winds

We Are Here, Though Our Glory Be Brief

I've seen them wedged in narrow cracks, these tiniest of plants pushing their way between dusty red rocks, their succulent leaves clustered at their feet, each no larger than a piñon nut, yet hoarding water to last the season, channeling energy up to feed a swarm of miniature buds—pendulous yellow bundles hanging on in high altitude winds, racing each other to the sky—and they've got the stamina, they know what eager means, they don't stop reaching for the sun, for they haven't much time, they have to do it all in the space of one short summer, and I wish I could hear them when they unfurl, I wish I could be there when they sing!

Air Songs

The air is singing again—
      its hum   an underground current
         its voice   a shapeshifter.

     At dawn   it seems a pale vibration
       a seeping crescendo
as the steadfast sun breaches the horizon.

        Later it soars like an aria—
     high-luster tones   reverberate   resonate
          shine and ring
      with a blue-sky timbre.

Lungs full of laughter it runs hand-in-hand
     with the dancing stream
         joins with ranks
      of shimmering aspen—

  a chorus of wind-driven voices
      quivers like a choir
         of leaf tambourines.

A bass line surges   tossing the trees.
    In pulsing rain a relentless rumble
       intensifies
                hovers
       drops to a tremor.

       As dusk dims   notes flicker
         like fireflies of sound—
  their traces subside
          sink into shadow.

The air is singing again—

               tonight it whispers
          to the half-hidden moon—
                      a hymn that intones
               the silence of stars.

Storehouse

As late summer flirts with early autumn,
Earth tries to feed us with her bounty

like an aproned grandmother—*Here, have another helping,
you're so thin, put some meat on those bones,*

you must store enough excess to last the winter.
Excess what, I wonder.

What will I collect like acorns to bury
as my cache, what morsels will sustain me?

I store up ribbons of unstructured days that flow
like a river's meander, strands of calm to weave

a cushion for my spirit, and pockets of patience
to stitch into the lining of my winter coat.

I gather the voices of dear friends to strengthen
my own, and enough words to speak to each day

in its own language. In fields of time
I harvest hours ripe for dancing,

and to light my way I wrap myself
in the golden shimmer of summer's waning.

Pomegranate

I carve five slits around its crest
                etch down its leathery sides
pry one segment from another

clusters of potential nestle within

from the heart of this crimson orb
                kernels of possibility spill
across my cutting board

their sheen emits a glow—
                a tincture of light stealing
through the crack in tomorrow's door

I harvest these nascent worlds
                a few already fallen into decay
soft and browning
                like ideas that need to die

others—firm packets of promise—
                erupt with the juice of desire

seeds of creation
                they do not tell the future
they only taste like it

Where Do All the Colors Go

As blues intensify above—

        before they fade
                      to winter white—

we crush the russet underfoot

            along with marigold and dusty
      orange
                  grind them   with the red
       of brick.

But where's the verdant green?

        November swaddles it with cold

              and cradles it
   within the earth   to birth
                              again

       in fertile spring.

Talking with Trees

In the after-snowfall silence I listen
        to the bare trees of winter,

lean in to hear their wisdom whisper—
        this is the best time

to scan the patterns of your growth,
        decide which branches need pruning,

which offshoots are heading
        in the wrong direction.

In the spring,
        I will ask these trees how

to stretch my arms wide,
        hold myself up to the sky,

allow the furled layers of my heart
        to unfold like leaves—

how to use every inch of this openness
        to break down toxins,

transform the air and exude
        something beneficial,

something to help all those around me
        breathe.

Doggedness

That's what really gets me—the doggedness of it,
the tightened-core determination, the grit of these
slender, still-tightly-wrapped daffodil buds waving
their coming yellowness in the face of persistent
gray skies, nothing surrounding them but bare dirt,
and it's the same with these pale old-rose hellebores,
their feet mired in last year's leaves—looking just
like us when the cold closed us down, kept us from
moving freely, ankles awash in our own wintry debris—
but there they are, daring to show up in biting March
winds, their chins tucked in a perpetual fight against
the chill, yet still their mouths open to speak—

> *Don't worry, it's early in the game yet, we know*
> *this fledgling spring fails to fill you with warmth*
> *and light and blue-sky clarity, but remember—*
> *we are here, offering our tenacity as a promise*
> *to fight for whatever beauty there is to be had.*

Sakura

Expecting to see only azaleas
—Tokyo's spring coming early this year—

I round the bend in the strolling garden

and stop—

eyes fixed   on an enormous
flowering tree

masses   of miniature clouds
cascade
from its branches
billows of
spilled powder pink
tumbling
excess

ruffled puffballs
of swirling fluff   become
double blossoms dense
with delicate folds
layers of petals
cradled within petals
painted
against the sky
in thick strokes   as though
with a palette knife

and there I stand
no longer a visitor
but a witness   in the midst
of a centuries-old tradition—

cherry blossom viewing.

II. Threshold

Fern Room, Lincoln Park Conservatory

Pungent odors of root-rich soil permeate
still air.　　A warm dampness　　seeps
through dense vegetation　　water
slips over rocks　　a soothing murmur.

Cushioned moss　　creeps through cavities
etched in sunken stone　　　　feathered fractal
leaves of miniature ferns reach out　　stroke
the skin. High overhead　　colossal cycads—

their massive fronds like shields—stand guard.
Shafts of light pierce through mottled
glass panes　　countless shades of green—
chartreuse　　emerald　　jade—flicker.

Beneath all movement
　　　an ancient energy pulses.

　　　*******

Fiddlehead coils　　stretch　　　unfurl
their limbs like dancers　　awakening.
Tendrils of Spanish moss—strands
of tangled　　iridescent hair—tickle

the cheek that brushes against them.
Indeterminate sounds emerge　　hollow
random　　the low hum of primeval souls
as they pass through thick　　shadows.

Surrounded by living walls   cradled
by a moving canopy   boundaries
between plants and limbs   earth and flesh
air and blood   become   tenuous.

An energy pulses   lower
    than the threshold of sound.

        ****

Humid air descends   enters
saturates each cell   the skin
a glistening membrane   the whisper
of one's heartbeat   slows with the breath.

Lulled into stillness   feet sink
into cool earth   eager vines circle
commence their ascent   wrap each ankle
and calf   inch upward to embrace

the thighs   caress the belly
a velvet moss   spreads
into secret places
the body   enveloped.

And deep within one's core
the pull of the earth   pulses.

In Search of Magic

inspired by the Chicago Botanic Garden

    We wend our way
along paths that wind
           through iridescent rooms
   of glass.
          Cascades of color
saturate us   and drape a cloak
   of exuberant chroma
        across our shoulders.

We can almost hear
        the whir of vibrating hues
that shimmer   in the moist air.
   Their murmuring tones   resonate
        like a thousand-voice choir
     humming a hymn
of enchantment.

        The air hangs heavy
           with blooming abundance.
   We sense a human echo beneath
       these floral faces
some   quietly elegant   others
   flamboyant and flirty all of them
        luminous.

Showering us   with the succulence
   of translucent petals and sepals
          they whisper
     their delicate mystery
and spill seduction from their lips
        as we stand speechless
   among the orchids.

The Statue in the Orchid House Becomes My Teacher

inspired by Chicago's Lincoln Park Conservatory

She stands with bent head,
      both hands grasp a burden
that bears down on her shoulder—
      a vessel of heaviness that seems immovable.
I fear its weight might tear
her thin garment of stony protection.

Yet as I approach, I hear her say,
      There is much you do not know,
            much that I can teach you.
      My head is not always bowed
            over the placid pool below.

      I inhale the perfume of Madagascar vanilla
            on the day it chooses to bloom.
      I feel the tickle of whiskered koi
feeding around my ankles.

I can hear distant music
      that caresses my limbs,
softens marble to flesh,
      releases my earthbound feet.

Each night I set down my urn and dance
      with the orchids,
      their colorful gaiety—my own.

She speaks again, her words
        finding their echo in my voice—

Each day I can choose
to lift my burden again
       yet still say no to it.

Threshold

after Joan Fullerton's mixed media collage "Beyond the Gate"

glimpses
     of possibilities
  beckon us
     across the threshold
    toward what is yet unclear
       where barren branches
    will burst into leaf
      nature's patterns
    will fill our pores
        white light
     will spill color at our feet
      and the poppies
   we know are there
         will dance into focus
   and bequeath us their joy

Walking Meditation

matching the pace of others
I circle out
through revolving doors
settle into a rhythmic stride
release all thoughts
into some vast
holding space above the April sky
senses open
sounds begin to seep in
pulsing hum of bicycle wheels
pad of runners' footfalls
overlapping cadences of conversation
shrill tones of children mingle
with cries of seagulls
and always
the drone of lakeshore traffic
eyes assimilate
the bobbing of joggers' bodies
the crisscross darting
of dogs playing catch
cyclists weaving with fluid grace
a soundless scull glides through the harbor
and always
ribbons of cars stream at the edges of sight
feet respond as pavement changes
to ragged surface
of quarried stone steps
my body absorbs
warmth of wind
pale perfume of forsythia
earthy taste of air after rain
alert to each nuance
yet focused
on none

Hidden Knowledge

As I drive north on I-25, light slips into dark,
the mountains to my left rendered as strips of color—
deep dusty indigo fading to the far peaks of pale
blue-stained gray. They seem but a veiled backdrop—

and yet my body knows what secrets they conceal
behind this façade fashioned by dusk and distance.
> *My eyes still see the willow-lined valley*
> *that wakes under pillows of persistent mist,*
> *and my senses know that tomorrow a bevy*
> *of birds will sing the sun into the sky.*

Inside the Jeep, as I half-listen to the hum of Denver traffic,
> *my ears can still hear hail pelting the Big Blue Trail,*
> *can catch the cries of coyotes rejoicing over their kill,*
> *the scrabbling of rock chucks running on stubby legs,*
> *the soft staccato hoot of owls.*

Even as I tighten my hold on the steering wheel
and my foot dances between brake and accelerator,
> *in my mind I run my hands along pockmarked*
> *granite boulders laced with lichen. My soles feel*
> *the cushioned layers of decomposing forest,*
> *soft and springy underfoot.*

The light on the interstate fades, yet somehow
> *my eyes trace the supple curve of a fisherman's fly line,*
> *and my bones feel the rhythmic beating of the earth*
> *as a herd of elk trots single file into the trees.*

From this distance the slopes are silent—
all they harbor, hidden. Yet even
at this hour, on this highway, still
> *my body remembers.*

A Language of Sensing

inspired by The Morton Arboretum's mission
"where people and trees thrive together"

You can run your hand along the deep ridges
and furrows of the white ash—
let your skin read it as though it were Braille.

Your mouth might relish the sweetness
of linden leaf buds—bundled leaves
murmuring their tender messages.

If you linger in a stand of white pine—
inhale their healing fragrance—
they will tell you of their essence.

Cottonwoods borrow the wind's voice to whisper
through their big-hearted leaves—while aspen
sing along in a shake-and-shuffle dance.

And look at the sugar maple—draped
in autumnal robes it declares itself to your eyes
as it will later in its full winter nakedness.

Our senses know—already—how to speak
with these sentinels of the plant world.
Perhaps when we practice this language

something even deeper within us
will commune with the trees.

Undercurrents

*dedicated to Five Element acupuncturist,
Melissa Farran*

My eyes feast on the suppleness
      of the sea, its pulsing ripples pushed
and prodded by wind, the way
      its shadows shift as they dance,
its skin dappled with dozens
      of whitecaps flashing signals
from the sun. At that moment
      when a wave's thin ridge tips
and folds and falls like snow,
      I focus on its height, its crest and trough,
its frothing aftermath—this textured
      surface we can see—yet all this time
I know that underlying currents
      feed the ocean's breath.

Why do I forget that power forms
      in shadowed depths,
and builds its strength
      where it can grow unseen?

I think about all this while lying
      on the acupuncture table,
where the point is not what happens
      to this outer sheath of skin—
the focus is to find those hidden
      crossroads where energy channels
intersect, to clear their flow, allow them
      to align. Beyond the prick I wait
for that deeper hit, a sudden ache,
      a palpable heat that spreads,
that tells me something has opened,
      a fire has been stoked.

Learning from Landscape

after Joan Fullerton's painting "Sedona Speaking"

sometimes

       all that surrounds us
           is all that we need—

  packed red earth to buttress our feet

           sagebrush to show us
       how to withstand wind

slabs of rock to remind us of a few solid truths

      and in the distance   one jagged hill
         to demonstrate persistence

         despite time's erosion

Promises Made by a Chinese Landscape Painting, When You Enter at Its Feet

after a series of ink paintings by Lo Cheng-Hsien

```
                        sky
                    the
             as they offer you
                    to you of strength
             their stillness will speak
     with their steadfast arms
             they will shield you
     give your gaze to my mountains

             the courage to embrace them
     my clouds will carry your dreams    until you gather
             upward        regardless of the terrain
I will teach you to always move forward
                                        of my paths?
                    the steepness
     why do you see only

                    into the breath of clear vision
             they will not veil your senses    but transform them
                    that settle on my slopes?
do you fear you will lose your way in the mists

             their surface will reflect    whatever light you need
     my streams    will smooth your turbulence with song

             across the waters    of your worry
     my bridge will lay a platform of calm

             my rivers will rinse time from your pockets
the hush of my forest    will drown out your noise

                            you can rest here
             Enter    if you will
```

Against a Bleached Evening Sky

these gulls tonight
swoop in formation
switch direction in flight—morph
from thin pale jottings to become
a swirl of strong dark strokes

                        these gulls tonight
                        fly with a pulsing rhythm
                        wingtip to wingtip—one entity—
                        synchronous motion imprinted
                        in their cells

    and what of us—will we rise
    and plunge and rise again together
    fingers reaching to sense the other's trajectory
    the two of us breathing as one
    inhaling each other
    exhaling all else?

Skybound

If in the end
you and I
my friend
sail
too close to the sun
singe
our bright wings and
plummet
to the land of mere
mortals
let us not dwell
on the smell of burnt
flesh
but rather
on the fragrant air
of our ascent.
And let us not strew
the ocean with ash,
but rather let the sea
be adorned
with pearls we pulled
from the sky.

Aubade

a half moon hovers
        a quiet observer on a backdrop of blue
I, too, make no sound
            as the warm breeze skims my cheek
    ruffles the tufted crest
      of the nearby cardinal's cocked head

the birds have long since begun
        their conversations

a mourning dove's cooing to lure a mate
    the shrill call of a chickadee
          sounding an alarm—hawk overhead
    the cardinal's strong whistle
        staking out his territory

their language is not mine

nor do I have wings to help me catch
        a column of air
    nor hollow bones to render me
            almost weightless

and yet this morning
        as I leave the moon behind

I try to coax a column of light
      to fill my thirsty bones
    I watch my spirit start to rise
          on this day's updraft

and I begin to summon this song
        to claim the whole wide sky
    as my terrain

III. Inhaling Light

Across the Water

after Joan Fullerton's painting "Moonlight Yearning"

a chill
recedes
as fire—
kindled
from slivers
of hope birthed
by the moon—
reaches
from one
shore
to another
and light
speaks
to light

Solstice Promise

Night unrolls its thickness
        across this dormant ground   envelops
            trunks of sugar maple   oak
and birch   oozes between the slats
      of cedar fencing   obliterates
           the neighboring house.   My vision
cannot penetrate its density   and yet I know
      that somewhere   the sun still lives
          still offers its rays of luminosity.

On days when I observe
      some other kind of darkness   unroll
        across my mind   shroud my thoughts
and stain my tongue   still   I sense
      a certainty   vibrating
        beneath the shadows
a recognition that light   will never leave me
      that light lives always
        somewhere   deep within.

Inhaling Light

Today asthma
      embeds itself in my chest
           breathing labored
moving at a measured pace
      I take my lungs
           for a walk
inhale light
      with every sun-soaked step
           hoping
light can substitute for breath.
      My chest opens to radiance
           wherever I can find it—
the dancing surface
      of a glitter-spangled pond
           a sudden gleam
as sunlight strikes white-breasted geese
      the sky itself as it shimmers
           with incandescence.
My lungs gather glistenings
      from the farmers market—
           the glimmering flesh
of black raspberries
      the sheen of cherry skins
           the golden luster of apricots.
Ambling through the conservatory
      I collect light from unexpected sources—
           quiet koi with flares of orange
flashing from their scales
      and water lilies that emit
           a yellow luminescence.
I even breathe in the sparkle in a young girl's eyes
      as she rubs the velvet underbelly
           of ginger leaves.

As I absorb reflections flaming
      from the fountain's bronze cattails
          brilliant rays that leap
from greenhouse glass
    and shards of sunlit fire
        glinting off the lake
I let my lungs gorge on light.

It All Happens Here

The right lung is made up of three lobes.
The left lung has only two lobes to make room for your heart.
                                        —healthline.com

It all happens here,
        at this crossroads, this place
                of exchange,
where we trade one thing for another,   leave
                                            behind
whatever is waste   in our lives,   then
            gather in
        whatever we need.

                You picture, perhaps, only a few square inches
                        of contact,
                where heart nestles next to lungs.

But get this . . .
        clusters of tiny air sacs
            called alveoli   perch
at the end
        of each bronchiole tube—about
                six hundred million alveoli,
            with a surface area
equivalent to the size of a tennis court.

We're not talking about a few bunches
        of miniature grapes here.

                      And each alveolus
          is covered by a network of capillaries.   That's
              where the handoff takes place.

Think about it . . .
>> the heart
> can give up its debris
>> of anger,
discouragement,
> loneliness,

> can gather up
> the pieces   of its grief, spill them
into blood flowing
> through these microscopic tributaries,
send all of it   to the lungs.

>> The lungs corral
> these discarded toxins,
>> bundle them with carbon dioxide,
>>> then expel
>> the whole mess.

Look what happens next . . .
> these same 300,000 square inches
>>> of connection
infuse the bloodstream with oxygen,
> imbue it
>> with healing,
enable the lungs   to cradle the heart.

Inner Body

At first I found it easy
to perceive this body
as some tactile thing,
composed of joints
and tendons, organs, fluids,
pathways made of veins.

And so a knowing came—
that I must work
this body, build
its strength, dance
my limbs to suppleness.
A focus on the tangible.

Yet over time I learned
this temporal structure
built of bone and flesh
protects a vast internal
force that nourishes
the spirit's muscle tissue.

I had to go beyond
the body, come
full circle and return
to offer it my gratitude
for guarding
what goes on inside.

Putting My Mind Down for a Nap

With a gentle
touch I take
my mind
by the hand
stroke
its frayed surface
coax
it to breathe
from its belly
hoping
I can calm
its quivering.

I soften
my voice
to speak to it
tell my mind
I respect
its thoughtful
analysis
its ability
to process
information
its initiative—even
its propensity
to go its own way—

but I need it
to disappear
for a while.
So I lay it
with care
on a padded surface
cover it
with a queen-size
down comforter
and tuck it in
all the while
humming
a few bars of
James Taylor's
You Can Close Your Eyes.

Murmuring
reassurances
that I will soon
return to rescue it
I turn
from my mind
to notice
the newly open
space within
and watch
as it fills with light.

Wick

When everything within me
            slumps
        like a wilting hydrangea
          in ninety degree heat,
when my whole self   shrinks
         and curls inward
      like the leaves of a parched dogwood,
when I feel my fortitude hanging low
          to the ground—
      the branches of my being
scraping the dirt   until I fear they will snap
         into dry kindling,

I try to remember to look deeper.

I let my hand take hold of the slender-tipped
       blade of self-kindness.   I lift
a sliver of my protective bark and slice
       into my core— sometimes in my chest
close to my heart   or perhaps in the soft belly
         of my soul.

I close my eyes to sense any greenness there.
       It takes time   for the color to morph
         from deadwood brown
      to a more vibrant hue.
As a hint of verdancy begins to emerge,
     I take tiny sips of it   suck
        on its moisture until it seeps
     into unseen pores.

Signs of life   though subtle and veiled—
      my spirit is wick.

Wakening

In response to a painting by Tania Blanco, "Healer of the Soul"

*There's a crack in everything.
That's how the light gets in*
—Leonard Cohen

My spirit lies fallow—
a barren plot of parched ground,

an abandoned lot hemmed in by walls
that feed my darkness. In the shadows

a flute begins to play. Notes flicker and fade
like fragments of ancient music—familiar,

though I've never heard it before.
I sense movement,

a shift in the flow of air, a trail
of warmth along my wounds.

The music strengthens, seeps
into inner crevices, teases out

strands of my forgotten song.
Notes shape themselves

into droplets of water, form a trickle,
grow into rivulets that run

through thirsty cracks. They find
those seeds of wholeness hidden within,

soften them until they split,
sending green shoots skyward.

My spirit leafs out,
breathing in the light.

Musings on the Body

Despite all the music in the air
the only rhythm that matters
    is the breath of the body.

Straddling two worlds
the body is born
    of Earth's fire
    coupled
with all the sound waves
    from the stars.

They say the body is mostly water.
When the body descends into sleep
    it feels the tide-pull
    of many oceans.

They say the body is mostly space.
When sky sings through its open corridors
    the body dances.

Perhaps the body is mostly music—
    the bass notes of bones
    the cadence of flesh
    the whole body humming.

When a storm comes
and turbulent winds echo the chaos
    the body offers shelter.

In its hidden passages —
    where Earth's heat meets
    with ether's cool air—
the body's murmur mingles
    with the galaxy's breath.

Paradelle for La Loba

> La Loba *sings over the bones. To sing means to use the soul-voice to breathe soul over the thing that is in need of restoration.*
> —Clarissa Pinkola Estés in *Women Who Run With the Wolves*

Singing life and energy into the bones with her breath,
singing life and energy into the bones with her breath,
she dances as silent drumming speaks the sun's rising.
She dances as silent drumming speaks the sun's rising.
And rising, the sun's energy speaks, drumming the bones
into life, as she with her silent breath singing, dances.

In the glade, beneath the moss, my feet like roots caress the earth.
In the glade, beneath the moss, my feet like roots caress the earth.
Standing, waiting in the wind, I would listen for her song.
Standing, waiting, in the wind I would listen for her song.
I, like the earth, waiting for roots beneath, standing in the glade,
caress the moss. Her song in the wind—would my feet listen?

Veins of a deep river run laughing in rich, red rock.
Veins of a deep river run laughing in rich, red rock.
My soul gathers water, clear and calm it feeds my flesh.
My soul gathers water clear and calm—it feeds my flesh.
My red veins of rock run calm and deep, my flesh
gathers soul in a rich river. Clear, laughing water feeds it.

Her energy rising, she speaks in song like the breath
of the wind, silent beneath deep drumming. Listen—
for in the glade, rich moss gathers life, waiting feeds
her calm roots, water would clear my veins. The sun's a red rock
standing in the river, and my soul—it dances! And with flesh
singing into bones, my feet caress the earth as I run, laughing.

Evidence of Fire

this Earth
        whose hills beckon   like a homecoming
            whose fields
      lie golden and greening at my feet
her rolling contours   packed
            with sustenance

in her heart
        she guards   a molten core
            sends its heat   upward
nourishing growth   across her surface

she breathes her fire
            into my own belly
it fills my pores   flares
        in my eyes   flashes
      from my footsteps

as I roam the landscape
                of her outer crust
      with its thin layer   of life

IV. The Calm Embedded in Forward Motion

Riverspeak

after Veronica Patterson

First, I must speak of whispering my troubles to the stones,
how their churning foam washes away my agitation.

But I also speak of whatever the water whispers to me—
the rippling tongue of its movements, the cadence
of its currents, teaching me to flow unfettered.

I speak of the conversation between us—the river's
speech spills into my veins, soothes my pulses, its language
swells, subsides, its murmurs echo my own.

I will let the rivers speak their own names—Roaring Fork,
Big Sandy, Brandywine, Cascade, Whitewater, Blue Earth,
Stillwater, Wind.

All of this speaks of the comfort of constant
changefulness, slipstreams running past quiet pools,
the calm embedded in forward motion.

Pilgrimage, Early March

Only a short walk, one taken each year.
I leave behind my mind's chatter,
step into the courtyard, make my way
across half-buried slabs of stone
to the path of moss-lined bricks, leading

to one particular patch of the garden
with its bare canes of black raspberry,
the winter remains of daylilies.
A few stray stalks of peonies wave
above a field of dried stubble.

I kneel in the cushion of ivy, a strata
of vines laid down over decades. A glimpse
of the telltale white of early bloodroot—
its flower still bound tightly—
but this is not the sign I seek.

In front of my bowed head—a mound of brittle
brown leaves left over from autumn's drift
and caught in the tangled debris. My hand knows
to brush them aside, my quick intake of breath
heralds these acolytes of spring,

these clusters of fleshy green sedum buds
huddled to give each other strength.
Each one a bundle of succulent leaves.
Each year somehow knowing how
to make their way toward the light.

Horizon

after Joan Fullerton's painting "Toward the Horizon"

I build this path
        out of fragments   gleaned
    from life's riverbed
          laid down
      as flagstones

    each day's colors
        like swaths
      of dappled shadow   and light
        strewn
            across the years

      shards that crystallize
          into a kaleidoscope of beauty

            each new patch of ground
        a foothold   leading
          to that still-distant
                    half-hidden
              horizon

Bhutan—Notes from a Journey

5th day, 4th temple

At Jampa Lhakhang   we slip off shoes
leave them on stone steps   pull aside
the fiercely colored cloth curtaining   the doorway
step over—not on—the seventh century threshold
onto burnished wood worn   polished
a patina from thousands of bare feet.
Rainbows of color burst from exuberant textiles
incense   strong but not sweet
the smell of butter from the butter lamps.

6th day, 11th temple

Our daughter and the two monks traveling with us
make their prostrations. Offering of money in hand
we touch it to our foreheads   lay it on an altar filled
with flowers   fruits   food   flanked by two elephant tusks.
The caretaker monk lifts an elegant vessel
the thinnest of spouts peacock feather adorning its lid
pours a small puddle of sacred water into my cupped hand.
I take a sip   spread the rest on my head.
One of the monks begins to explain the stacked images
of gods   painted   on every inch of wall.

Deities   myriad reincarnations of deities
a multitude   of manifestations
some benevolent   some angry   multiple gurus
arhats [what are arhats?]
the bodhisattvas   [spelling?]
countless forms of Padmasambhava,
more variations than the arms of Chenrezig—
that deity sometimes seen with eleven heads
a thousand arms   an eye in every palm.
Our guide called him Avalokiteśvara.
I finally learned how to say that—and it rolls off the tongue
rather nicely, doesn't it? A-va-lo-ki-tesh-va-ra.
And I figured out that Padmasambhava—
the one who brought Buddhism to Bhutan—
is the one they're calling Guru Rinpoche—"precious
teacher"—and I remember that Milarepa is a poet
but I've lost track—who is Pema Lingpa?

7th day, 17th temple

Always move clockwise
always   behind each altar   golden statues
always three important ones   different in every temple
sometimes Sakyamuni   the Buddha

and I know he's here   I see the coiled hair.
I've learned to recognize the next one, too
founder of Bhutan   Zhabdrung Ngawang Namgyal
the third one? I've no idea.
Surrounding them   a semi-circle of more statues
every detail significant   how each body is positioned
their garments   what they're sitting on
their mudra   or hand gesture. Once again
walls packed with paintings   the storytelling begins.

Gods   more gods   demigods   demons
depictions of local protective deities, too—
trying to make sense   I sink in this lake of—

It's all too much for me—this complex pantheon.

8th day, 18th temple

Punakha   so many surfaces coated in gold.
Today our monks—by now our friends—are wearing
their finest—sweeping red robes   generous drape
of orange scarf   and on their chests   bright sparks
of the royal yellow signify   their high ranking.

The stories continue   miracles   bigger than life
stories that require putting aside doubt
suspending disbelief.

8th day, 21st temple

—the weight of it all—
still I bend my head to his quiet voice
try to listen   to follow   to pull something out
something to grasp   words that might form
stepping stones   so I can make my way
to temple   after temple
without drowning in the detail.

Then   as he speaks   from the heart
of Buddhist thought   three pillars rise
the first one   gratitude
to all who help   along the way
and then   loving-kindness
to those whose paths intersect with mine
the third   compassion
the eyes to see another's pain.

As I step outside of yet one more temple
I slip one foot into the shoe   of gratitude.

Prayer Ghazal

In a land like Bhutan where the wind reads the prayers
does the zephyr smell sweeter once the air's freed the prayers?

At high mountain passes fly squares of bright cloth
stamped in ink with requests—printed words plead the prayers.

The tall flags in white like frayed ragged feathers,
on hillsides they huddle like slim reeds—the prayers.

The hopes of the children, desires of the lonely,
the yearning of pilgrims, they all seed the prayers.

All the voices inside, all the words in your head
form earnest petitions—their noise feeds the prayers.

But when the whole lot needs healing, we fall to our knees.
It just doesn't matter who leads the prayers.

If I bow here in stillness, I honor the grief
of those who are mourning, whose hands bleed the prayers.

As silence diffuses through layers of sorrow
I find myself asking—do none heed the prayers?

I must learn to look up, teach my heart how to kneel
Call me *one among many,* for we all need the prayers.

Trying on Cultural Symbols in Taipei

I know nothing of auspicious dragons—
their image does not appear over the centuries
in the art of my ancestors. I gaze up
at these daunting sentinels—their fierce mouths,
brilliant blue bodies, sweeping tails—
for generations shielding Longshan Temple.
Perhaps I too could be safe within the curves
of their serpentine scales. I can picture them
crouched on the roof of my heart,
battling evil spirits, banishing them
to some place where they cannot hurt me.
I begin to see sorrows swept away, clasped
in the claws of these big-hearted beasts.

And if I picture the sun rising
on the back of a bird, perhaps
I would live that day with more light
rising inside me, would feel its wings
carry me above the concerns of the day.
To begin the morning
with that much significance
can hardly be a bad thing.

All around me I see the crane—that emblem
of long life—elongated neck, endless
legs, extension of black-tipped wings—
a bird that knows how to make the journey.
Yet instead of calling on these cranes
to grant me a multitude of days, perhaps
these expert dancers could teach me how
to move with grace through whatever days I have.

But what do I do with the Chinese phoenix—
that mythical fusion of multiple animals,
multiple birds, multiple meanings?
I lose my way here—but I do recall
one of the five virtues living in the five colors
of its tail feathers—a reminder to leave
benevolence in my own wake.

Call and Response

*I want to be improbable beautiful
and afraid of nothing, as though I had wings.*
—Mary Oliver

This ocean of life calls my name and I
must answer with full voice. I want
its every dawn to find me dancing to
the rhythm of its waves, though it may be
their undertow engulfs me. For joy—so improbable—
will surface, bathing the shores of this sea—so beautiful,
so redolent with fragrant glory, yet often cruel and
always ephemeral. There is no time to be afraid,
to clutch at safety and miss the chance of
diving into shadows, climbing to the light, nothing
held back. My heart wades in even as
the tide's muscled grip seizes me, even though
it drags me into deep waters. When strength is spent, I
will lift my face to the horizon and—grateful to have had
this voyage—take to the sky with salt-studded wings.

Shoreline

Along this rim of the Pacific   I breathe
    with the sea's rise and fall   my pulse
        echoes its rhythmic surge.
Feet flex with these sands   dense
    yet undulating   a ground that shifts
        when liquid power pours out upon it.
Piercing calls of shore birds   the roll and rumble
    of whitecaps   a soft exhale
        as this giant body of water recedes.

Rocky tidepools harbor rippling anemones
    a rainbow of sea stars.
        The ocean's pounding oscillations
leave behind   gelatinous strands of seaweed
    driftwood fragments   abandoned shells.
        A shoreline that accepts what the tides bring in.

Isn't this what my body must do—
    absorb whatever breaks
        upon it wave after wave?
It forms its own tidepools—   pockets
    that shelter   sorrow   joy
        passion   pain.
I have heard this body keen
    with the winds   cry
        with the plaintive voice of gulls.
Sometimes it sits   in silence
    letting life's questions
        wash over it.

Isn't this body called upon
····to hold
············the immensity of life—its storms
its fierce loves·······its calm interludes?

····And just like the shoreline
············when it reaches deeper
it becomes··········the sea floor—
······strong enough
············to cradle·····the world's cadence.

Each Moment a Bird

Time disguises itself
        as a boundless swath of sky
no hard edges   no distinct
        beginning or end   glowing
with eternity's formless light.

Yet if I use the "Now"
                to fashion a lens
      I focus each ray
burn each present moment
        into being.

                Each one
flames into view like a bird
        flashing by   each one
emerging from the ether   each one
        calling out   "This is What Is."

But if—instead—my eyes crave the future

I will search the heavens in vain
                for winged creatures
        all the while deaf
to the birdsong   resounding
        in this firmament.

Metamorphosis

This day
               curled in my lap

                            wants to be stroked.

    One breath of time
                      that hangs
            like tender fruit

          beckons   like a ripe pear.

I press my lips against its moist flesh.

                It morphs
   into stone
                    then wind
         then meadow.

Conversation with Bashō

*No one travels
Along this way but I,
This autumn evening.*
　　—Matsuo Bashō

Other travelers have
journeyed here,
the same moon rising.

I see their bits of wisdom scattered
along the roadside, opening
like evening primrose.

> Still, you are right, Bashō—
> I travel solo.
> Yet never alone.

The river's curves
encourage me
when my way is not straight.

These trees sing to me—
songs of resilience hum
within their roots.

> Like you, Bashō,
> this rhythm of nature
> is my cadence, too.

Tonight, stillness
of autumn dusk
settles on my shoulders.

Evening,
slipping in beside me,
holds my hand.

Belonging

I am not yet familiar
    with the ways of this land,
        not   like those who drink
    from its valleys   day
        after day,   who sit
    with its mountains evening
        after evening.

I want to understand its moods,
    its appetites, its attitudes,
        the way it sometimes holds
    you to its breast,   the way
at other times, it stands apart—
    aloof—accepting admiration
        from a distance.

How can I learn to listen to this land,
    to hear it tell me where
its water lives   and where
    it hides its fruits?

I want to know the scent
    of its arousal, the color
        of its anger
    and where its storms
        will go to die—

            to know what makes
                    the wildflowers waken,
            what level of light the hawks
                    need for hunting
                            and when the elk
            will agree to be seen.

If I sing to these forests,   perhaps
        they will show me how
                to read the signs of sickness
                        in their trees,
                to learn which creatures
                        whisper to the night
        and which ones dance
                        with the sun.

If I walk with these winds,
        I will hear the sound
                of leaves   letting go,
                    of snow
                caressing the river.
                    My eyes
        will read the surface of streams.

And as I live in these skies,
        my steps will span
                        their wild expanse,
        I will learn the language
                of birds.

About the Author

Melissa Huff explores free verse and metered poetry, enjoying the structure as well as the patterns of sound and rhythm inherent in both. She feeds her poetry from the power and mystery of the natural world and the ways in which body, nature, and spirit intertwine.

Her poem "Talking with Trees" garnered a 2024 Pushcart Prize nomination, while many of her other works have earned recognition in local and national contests. An advocate of the power of poetry presented out loud, Melissa twice won awards in the *BlackBerry Peach Prizes for Poetry: Spoken and Heard*, sponsored by the National Federation of State Poetry Societies (NFSPS). She has read her work at literary festivals and private parties, in bookstores, art galleries and classrooms, in coffee shops, pubs, museums and libraries, on Zoom, in an arboretum, and in the rotunda of New Mexico's State Capitol building.

Melissa's poetry has appeared in many journals, including *Blue Heron Review, The Orchards Poetry Journal, RockPaperPoem, Gyroscope Review, Persimmon Tree, Snapdragon: A Journal of Art and Healing,* and *Amethyst Review.* Several anthologies and other collections also include her work, such as *The Best of Halfway Down the Stairs, 2015–2019, Encore: Prize Poems 2022 (NFSPS),* Northern Colorado Writers' *Chiarascuro: Anthology of Virtue & Vice,* and *Thin Places & Sacred Spaces* from Amethyst Press.

Melissa is active with her workshop group, Plumb Line Poets, and enjoys membership in Poets & Patrons of Chicago, Lighthouse Writers in Denver, Colorado Poets Center, Illinois State Poetry Society, and Columbine Poets of Colorado. Having grown up in New Jersey and California, she now splits her time between Illinois and Colorado.

www.ingramcontent.com/pod-product-compliance
Lightning Source LLC
Chambersburg PA
CBHW030910170426
43193CB00009BA/797